PLEASE HANG UP

A One-Act Play

By

ARTHUR S. ROSENBLATT

THE DRAMATIC PUBLISHING COMPANY

****

ISBN 0-87129-107-X

This play is dedicated
in loving memory
to
John Sheridan Mintun.

PLEASE HANG UP

A One-Act Play
For One Man and Two Women, Extras

CHARACTERS

THOMAS T. TULLIS . . . . .A young bachelor

MRS. T (ULLIS) . . . . Tom's mother

JUDY . . . . Tom's prospective girlfriend

ASSORTED VOICES . . . . Extras

TIME: The Present
PLACE: The Apartments of Tom, Mrs. T. and Judy

PLEASE HANG UP

SCENE: The stage is bare except for three playing areas: DR is "Tom's Area;" UC is "Judy's Area;" and DL is "Mrs. T's Area."

AT RISE OF CURTAIN: A telephone rings in Tom's Area. The lights come up to reveal a red, pushbutton telephone next to an answering machine on top of a small table which also serves as a makeshift bar.

MACHINE. You have reached the telephone answering machine of Thomas T. Tullis, speaking to you on tape. I'm not here right now but if you'll please leave your name and telephone number, I'll get back to you as soon as possible. Thank you. (Beep tone, followed by the sound of a phone being slammed down. The lights go out in Tom's Area.)

(The lights come up in Mrs. T.'s Area. MRS. T. has just slammed down the receiver of a conventional black telephone on top of a small table covered with a red-checkered cloth.)

MRS. T. (speaking "at" the phone). Well, Mr. Fancy Pants, this is a mother speaking. A real person, with a voice. Thank you. Goodbye. (She exits and her lights go out.)

(The lights come up on Tom's Area as TOM enters. He looks at the answering machine, sees that there is a message, rewinds the tape quickly and plays the machine.)

MACHINE (after a buzzing sound). Please hang up. There appears to be a receiver off the hook. Please check your main telephone and extensions and try your call again. Thank you. This is a recording. (He stops the machine, somewhat disappointed, and pours himself a small scotch with a lot of water. He returns to the telephone and makes a call. Lights come up in Judy's Area as her phone rings. It is a pink princess telephone on a small white table next to a boudoir chair.)

MACHINE. Hi, this is Plaza seven, six, five, four, three. I really wish I were here to speak to you in person, but, oh well, I'm not. If you'd like to talk later, just leave your name and number at the sound of the beep tone and I'll get back to you as soon as I return. Remember, you just wait for that beep tone. And, hey, thanks for calling.

TOM. Well, hi, this is T.T.T. . . . or as you said, Mr. T-Cube. And you're not as sorry as I am that you're not there. But maybe next time. Okay? Catch you on the flip. Just wanted to let you know that I really enjoyed meeting you at the Watering Hole and – (The answering machine goes dead as the lights dim out on Judy's Area.) I finally got a job. (He hangs up the phone sadly and sips his drink, then dials another call. The lights come up on Mrs. T.'s Area. Her phone rings and rings but there is no answer. TOM hangs up his phone and dejectedly begins to remove his tie and shirt as he exits. The lights go down on Tom's Area.)

(MRS. T. enters her area with her head in a towel, a terry robe wrapped around her, dripping wet. She rushes to the phone, picks up the receiver, hears the dial tone and hangs up. She takes the towel off her head and wipes the floor. She looks at the phone for a moment, then dials. The lights come up on Tom's Area as his phone rings.)

MACHINE. You have reached the telephone answering machine of Thomas T. Tullis, speaking to you on tape. I'm not here right now but if you'll please leave your name and telephone number, I'll get back to you as soon as possible. Thank you. (A beep tone.)

MRS. T. So what's real soon? How soon? This is your mother. Better I should drown in the bathtub than you should stay home for five minutes. Someday you'll want something, then you'll answer the phone. Meanwhile, don't call for a half hour. I'm going to watch *Family Feud*. Goodbye, already. (She hangs up and exits. The lights on Mrs. T.'s Area go out.)

(The lights come up on Judy's Area as Judy enters, wiping crumbs from a chocolate chip cookie she is eating. She looks at her answering machine, sees a message, rewinds and presses the Play button.)

MACHINE. Well, hi, this is T.T.T. . . . or as you said, Mr. T-Cube. And you're not as sorry as I am that you're not there. But maybe next time. Okay? Catch you on the flip. Just wanted to let you know that I really enjoyed meeting you at the Watering Hole and – (There is a dial tone as the machine stops recording.) Please hang up. There appears to be a re-receiver off the hook . . . (Annoyed at the cutoff, JUDY stops the machine. She picks up her phone and presses the dial buttons. Offstage, there is a distant ringing.)

RHONDA (offstage). Hello out there. You have reached Rhonda Powers, but alas, not in the flesh. If you just leave your little old name and number, I'll do what I can to make you happy as soon as I can. Go ahead, tell me everything. You have thirty seconds.

JUDY (into the phone). Rhonda, it's Judy. You can't believe what just happened. Remember that kinda funny cute guy at the Watering Hole last night? He called and left a message, but no number, darn it. And I don't know how to get in touch with him. I know he lives on Horatio Street, but I didn't get his last name when he was talking to us. Did you? Give me a call and let me know, okay? 'Bye for now. (She hangs up the phone. Judy's Area lights go out. After a sustained pause, Tom's phone begins to ring as his lights come up.)

MACHINE. You have reached the telephone answering machine of Thomas T. Tullis, speaking to you on tape. I'm not here right now, but if you'll please leave your name and telephone number, I'll get back to you as soon as possible. Thank you.

RHONDA (offstage). Hi there, you sexy thing. This is the redheaded half of the dynamic duo from last night at the Watering Hole. Just couldn't face up to another night with one of the long list of desperados from my recent past, so if you're not busy tonight, why don't you give me a call. It's Rhonda, at Murray Hill six, one, four, one, eight. What have you got to lose that isn't already gone? 'Bye-'bye. (A click, then Tom's Area lights go out as the machine goes off.)

(Judy's Area lights come up. Judy paces back and forth, eating an apple, then goes to the phone and dials four, one, one.)

JUDY. Hello, Directory Assistance, you wouldn't have any way of finding the number of someone whose name is Thomas T. and then something or other that starts with a T, would you? On Horatio Street? (Directory Assistance obviously gives her a sharp rebuff. She looks astonished at the receiver and hangs up quickly as her area lights go out. She exits.)

(Mrs. T.'s Area lights come up as MRS. T. enters and dials fiercely. The lights come up in Tom's Area.)

MACHINE. You have reached the telephone answering machine of Thomas T. Tullis, speaking to you on tape. I'm not here right now, but if you'll please leave your name and telephone number, I'll get back to you as soon as possible. Thank you.

MRS. T. This is the voice of a person who would be richer by fifty thousand dollars if her name was Isabel Morales of Fresno, California, instead of Freida Tullis, formerly of Sheepshead Bay, now of Kips. It's also the voice of a mother who hopes she lives long enough to hear from her unemployed son to know if he got her CARE package. And a goodbye to you for now. I'm going next door to play Mah Jong. (She exits. Mrs. T.'s Area lights go out.)

(Judy's Area lights come up as JUDY walks in and looks at the machine. There are no messages. She picks up a magazine, puts it down, and dials the phone. A phone rings offstage.)

MALE VOICE (from offstage). Hello, this is the Ottoman Empire Deli. All our lines are busy right now, but if you'll hold on, our next available operator will be with you in a moment. Thank you for calling. (Middle Eastern belly dance music plays for a few seconds, then stops.)

FEMALE VOICE (from offstage). Ottoman Empire Deli. Can I help you?

JUDY (into the phone). Yes, I'd like a small order delivered, but I don't have much cash. Will you take a credit card?

FEMALE VOICE (from offstage). Minimum charge ten dollars.

JUDY (into the phone). I just want a sliced turkey on rye bread and a diet Dr. Pepper.

FEMALE VOICE (from offstage). Wait a minute. (Offstage, an adding machine works endlessly ringing up a vast array of numbers.) Just under. We can't deliver, but we can take it over the counter here.

JUDY (into the phone). Oh, all right, thank you. (She hangs up the phone, grabs her purse, and starts to exit, then she remembers the answering machine. She pushes the record button, crosses her fingers, turns and exits. After a brief pause, her phone rings.)

MACHINE. Hi, this is Plaza seven, six, five, four, three. I really wish I were here to speak to you in person, but, oh well, I'm not. If you'd like to talk later, just leave your name and number at the sound of the beep tone and I'll get back to you as soon as I return. Remember, you just wait for that beep tone. And, hey, thanks for calling.

DAVID DONALDSON (offstage). Hello, I had hoped to catch you at home. You probably haven't given much thought to planning for the future, but that's where I can be of help. That is . . .

(JUDY enters, clutching keys, panting and out of breath.)

MACHINE . . . David Donaldson of Fidelity Amalgamated Investment Corporation. I'd like to talk to you about a money market investment program so I'll try again in the near future. Thank you. (The machine stops. JUDY angrily presses buttons, then picks up the little microphone for a new message recording.)

JUDY (into the microphone). This is Judy. Just leave your name and number. No salesmen, please! (She slams down the microphone, pushes the record button and exits as her lights go out.)

(Tom's Area lights come up as TOM enters. He is dressed in jogging clothes and wearing a Walkman, including earphones. He goes to the answering machine, sees the message indications and is pleased. He takes out the recorded cassette and puts it in his Walkman and plays it while he does warm-up exercises. He scribbles down Rhonda's number and, after hearing all the messages, shuts off the machine. He takes off the earphones, goes to the phone and dials.)

MACHINE (from offstage). Hello out there. You have reached Rhonda Powers but alas, not in the flesh. If you just leave your little old name and number, I'll do what I can to make you happy as soon as I can. Go ahead, tell me everything. You have thirty seconds.

TOM (into the phone). Hello, Murray Hill, this is Greenwich. Sorry to disappoint you, but redheads aren't my thing. Besides, I already gave at the office. (He hangs up the phone, does another exercise or two, looks at his watch, then dials again. Judy's Area lights come up as her phone rings.)

MACHINE. This is Judy. Just leave your name and number. No salesmen, please.

TOM (surprised momentarily, but quickly rallying, into the phone). Well, the good news is that this isn't a salesman. No, it's me again, Mr. T-Cube, and I'm pleased to tell you that I just got a job as an account executive at an advertising agency. It's just a start, but someday you'll see it on the letterhead: "Benton, Bunton, Babcock, Butler and . . . (The line goes dead as recording time runs out and a hum comes on.) Tullis." I think we ought to abbreviate. Hey, are you out there? Oh, hell! (He hangs up, looks at his watch, and with a sigh of resignation, dials a new number. The lights come up on Mrs. T.'s Area as her phone rings continuously, with no answer. TOM hangs up, turns on his answering machine, puts on his headphones and exits, as his lights go out.)

(Mrs. T.'s phone stops ringing just as MRS. T. enters. She is obviously quite agitated. She presses a button on her telephone index, finds a number and dials the phone.)

MRS. T. (into the phone). Harriet? This is Frieda . . . Fine. Fine. I'm not fine. How can I concentrate on my melds when you can't hear yourself think from the ringing of this phone. The walls here are like toilet paper. Listen, how late is Max open tonight? . . . Huh? . . . Oh, good. Tell him not to close. I'll be right there. (She hangs up the phone, grabs her purse, starts to exit, then pauses. She goes back to the phone, starts to dial Tom's number, remembers, quickly hangs up and shakes her fist at the heavens.) A mother, a decent-minding-her-own-business mother, you have driven into the streets on a night like this. But look, who minds the expense? (She exits and her lights go out.)

(Tom's Area lights come on as he enters, wiping himself off with a towel. He checks his answering machine, sees no message indicated and decides to make a call. He dials the phone absent-mindedly while unlacing his sneakers.)

MALE VOICE (offstage, after a musical crescendo). You have reached the Magnificent Moussorgsky Chamber Ensemble. Our office is closed for the evening, but if you will please – (TOM quickly cuts off the mis-dialed number, but it has given him an idea. He picks up the newspaper, scans it for a moment, then carefully dials.)

FEMALE VOICE (offstage). This is Bloomingberg's Department Store. All our lines are tied up, but if you care to wait, one of our operators will be with you in a moment. (Music plays for a few seconds, then stops.)

OPERATOR. Bloomingberg's.

TOM. Good evening, may I have the ticket department, please?

OPERATOR. I'm sorry, those lines are busy right now. Would you care to hold or call back?

TOM. I'll hold.

OPERATOR. What tickets were you interested in purchasing?

TOM. Well, I'm looking for tickets to the Met.

OPERATOR. Which opera did you want?

TOM. Joan Sutherland in *Norma*.

OPERATOR. Are you kidding? You can't get near it. That's been SRO for a month. Why don'tcha try the ballet? My daughter-in-law, Grace, went last Tuesday and – (TOM cuts her off by hanging up. In total frustration, he turns on his answering machine and exits. Tom's Area lights go out.)

(Judy's Area lights come up as she enters and checks her answering machine. She plays back Tom's message as she unwraps her sandwich and distastefully removes the lettuce.)

MACHINE. Well, the good news is that this isn't a salesman. No, it's me again, Mr. T-Cube, and I'm pleased to tell you that I just got a job as an account executive at an advertising agency. It's just a start, but someday you'll see it on the letterhead: "Benton, Bunton, Babcock, Butler and – (The recording stops and the machine hums.) Please hang up. There appears to be a receiver off the hook. (Disappointed, JUDY takes a bite of her sandwich, then dials the phone.)

MALE VOICE (offstage). Hi, this is the Watering Hole. All our bartenders are busy right now, but if you care to wait – (JUDY slams the phone down angrily and starts to exit. Judy's Area lights go out.)

(Tom's Area lights come up as he enters, carrying a bowl of salad and eating pieces of lettuce with one hand. He looks at his watch, puts down his salad, goes to the phone and dials. Mrs. T.'s Area lights come up. Instead of the usual setting, there is a fancy, new, white one-piece trimline phone and a shiny new answering machine. The phone rings and the machine goes on.)

MACHINE (in a dignified tone). Hello, this is Butterfield eight, eight, zero, eight, zero, the residence of Frieda Teitelbaum Tullis. There's no one here right now, but you may leave a message which I will answer when I come back. When you hear the tone, go ahead, talk.

TOM (into the phone). Ma, you're terrific. I love you. Listen, I've got great news. I have a job and, if my lucky star is still shining, well, I've met Judy Miller, the girl of my dreams.

We're a perfect match. I'm still trying to get in touch with her, but just like you, she doesn't like to answer the telephone. Meanwhile, don't go anywhere, stay right where you are. You're in for a big surprise. (He hangs up and dials again as Mrs. T.'s Area lights go out. Judy's Area lights come up. The phone rings and Judy's machine goes on.)

MACHINE. Hi, this is Judy. Just leave your name and number. No salesmen, please.

TOM. Listen, it's Mr. T-Cube again. I have to go out, but I really want to talk to you. You can reach me at Butterfield eight, eight, zero, eight, zero. Goodbye, machine, I'm getting kind of fond of you. In a purely mechanical way, of course. (He puts down the phone and starts to leave, then has an idea. He stops and records a new message.) Hi, this is Tom. Just leave your name and number. Especially if it's Judy. (He exits and Tom's Area lights go out.)

(JUDY enters her area, eating a slice of pizza from a take-out carton. She checks her answering machine, sees that there's a message and plays it back.)

MACHINE. Listen, it's Mr. T-Cube again. I have to go out, but I really want to talk to you. You can reach me at Butterfield eight, eight, zero, eight, zero. Goodbye, machine, I'm getting kind of fond of you. In a purely mechanical way, of course. (JUDY dials the Butterfield number.)

(The lights come up on Mrs. T.'s Area as her phone rings. MRS. T. enters and answers the phone.)

MRS. T. (into the phone). Hello?

JUDY (into the phone). Butterfield eight, eight, zero, eight zero?

MRS. T. (into the phone). Yes.

JUDY (into the phone). Is . . . is Tom there?

MRS. T. (into the phone). No, you might say this is his answering service.

JUDY (into the phone). Oh. May I leave a message then? This is Judy Miller and he's been trying to reach me.

MRS. T. (into the phone). Oh, right. He left a message for you. He said to have you please meet him right away at one hundred forty-one Kips Bay Plaza, Apartment three-F. Come right up. The doorman will let you in because he'll have your name at the door. He said to rush. It's very important.

JUDY (into the phone). Really?

MRS. T. (into the phone). Would I lie? Could have something to do with his mother's health. She's practically a starving widow. That's all I know.

JUDY (into the phone). Well, thank you very much. (She hangs up. The lights go out on Mrs. T.'s Area and Judy's Area as BOTH exit. The lights come up on Tom's Area as his phone rings.)

MACHINE. Hi, this is Tom. Just leave your name and number. Especially if it's Judy.

FEMALE VOICE (offstage). Oh, dear me. I'm calling for the Village Eclectic Artists Association. I'm sure we must have a Judy somewhere on our membership list. Perhaps we'd best have her call you about a contribution to our fund-raising drive for the abolition of advertising signs on Village Walls. We'll be back to you real soon. (Tom's Area lights go out as Judy's Area lights come up. Her phone rings and the answering machine goes on.)

MACHINE. Hi, this is Judy. Just leave your name and number. No salesmen, please.

MALE VOICE (offstage). Hello, I'm not selling anything. I'm calling to tell you about a wonderful opportunity to get a bonus gift with a subscription to the *Gluttinous Gourmet* weekly magazine. This is a copy of *Instant Gratification*, our exciting new directory of fast-food franchises. To find out more about how to satisfy the hunger deep within, call us at Digest nine, one, eight, one, two. But hurry, this offer may be over any minute. (Judy's Area lights go out as Tom's phone rings and his lights go up.)

MACHINE. Hi, this is Tom. Just leave your name and number. Especially if it's Judy.

MALE VOICE (offstage, very gruff). This ain't no Judy. This is the Chambered Nautilus Health Emporium. We got a special going on and you're one of the lucky ones picked to take part. To get all the facts about finding the fun physique inside your flabby form, call us at Nautilus seven, three, seven, three, seven. Do it. Now. (Tom's Area lights go off as Judy's Area lights come up. Judy's phone rings.)

MACHINE. Hello, this is Judy. Just leave your name and number. No salesmen, please. (A pause, then just the sound of rather erotic, heavy breathing until the machine goes off and the hum comes on. Judy's Area lights go out. The stage is dark for a moment. Mrs. T.'s Area lights come up to reveal a table set with candles and a huge turkey, in front of the phone and answering machine.)

(TOM enters, pocketing his key and holding a huge bunch of flowers.)

TOM. Ma? Ma, are you home?

(The doorbell rings and TOM opens the door. JUDY stands in the doorway for a moment holding a bucket of Kentucky Fried Chicken. She enters the room and they look at each other in surprise. The phone rings and the answering machine goes on.)

MACHINE. Hello, hello. All right, I'm not there. But if you hear this, you are. And if you're both there and I'm not, what kind of message do I have to give you? There's a little something for a nibble, a little Mantovani on the phonograph and I've gone to the late show at the Orpheum. So what more are you waiting for? Listen to a mother for once instead of a machine. Please, please hang up. (The machine goes off. The lights go out.)

CURTAIN

DIRECTOR'S NOTES

DIRECTOR'S NOTES

DIRECTOR'S NOTES

DIRECTOR'S NOTES

DIRECTOR'S NOTES

DIRECTOR'S NOTES